DESPERATE
—— F O R ——
HAPPINESS
AND FINDING IT

DESPERATE

—— FOR ——

HAPPINESS

AND FINDING IT

Don L. Barfell

Library of Congress Control Number:		2016906114
ISBN:	Hardcover	978-1-5144-8517-0
	Softcover	978-1-5144-8516-3
	eBook	978-1-5144-8515-6

Print information available on the last page

Rev. date: 11/11/2016

To order additional copies of this book, contact:
Xlibris
1-888-795-4274
www.Xlibris.com
Orders@Xlibris.com
739074

Bible Citation

Scripture quotations marked KJV are from the Holy Bible, King James Version (Authorized Version). First published in 1611. Quoted from the KJV Classic Reference Bible, Copyright © 1983 by The *Zondervan Corporation*.

Scripture quotations marked NKJV are taken from the New King James Version. Copyright © 1982 by *Thomas Nelson, Inc*. Used by permission. All rights reserved.

DEDICATION

I am dedicating this book to my most wonderful family: my mother, my father, and my late wife, Susan, who are now in the presence of Christ; my three wonderful sons, Blair, Jason, and Justin; my daughter-in-law Kristy; my grandson Austin; and my granddaughter Averi.

ACKNOWLEDGMENTS

I would like to thank three very special friends, Bob
Moore Sr.,
Charlie Miller, and Kent Yoder, for their supportive Christian
knowledge
and their encouragement in helping me realize that it is with
God's help, in Jesus's
name, and through the power of prayer that one finds
true peace and happiness.

11 November 2007

I have struggled for the last eight years in putting my seventy-three years of life on paper. So here I go again! Not being educated in writing, I have asked for the Lord to help me in being able to put my life journey into words. My first thought was, it has been a life lived on a roller coaster car from the very first day I was born.

When God created man, he was so kind to have given each one of us a choice on how we want to live our lives. I believe most of us have lived through many valleys and mountaintop experiences in our lives. Some of these experiences last for a long time, while others last for just a short time. They are just part of our daily routine whether we like it or not, no matter how we live or how long we live. Our stay on this earth can end at any time without warning.

These experiences happen to each of us whether we are Christians, believing in Jesus Christ, or non-Christians, not believing in Christ. We all must live through them even if we do not want to. The question lies on how we choose to live through them. So why would we not want to live through these trials with the confidence and a sense of peace, which can only be had through a personal relationship with Christ?

Scripture tells us that when God created the earth, it was created with mountain peaks and valleys. It's these high mountain peaks and low valleys that have induced me to tell my life story.

After nine months in the making, orchestrated by my mother and father, I began my life journey at five pounds seven ounces and seventeen inches long—small by worldly standards. This all happened on July 19, 1942, in the town of Elkhart, Indiana.

Three weeks later, my father, who was working for Bendix Corporation, a company that was vital in supplying airplane engine parts at the time we were at war with Japan, was transferred to Omaha, Nebraska, in the cold winter of '42.

It was on that long drive that I developed pneumonia and was blessed to have survived such a trip.

After the war was over, we moved back to Goshen, Indiana.

As far as I know, up until that time, my life was normal for a six-and-a-half-year-old boy.

It was time for the first grade, and I was excited to begin. My older brother and I attended the same elementary school. While I was well into the first grade, my brother often let me ride me on his bicycle's handlebars to school, which was always a great thrill for me. This was until one morning when another boy came from out of nowhere and crashed into the side of my brother's bike, throwing me off headfirst on the payment.

The next thing I remembered was waking up some six hours later in bed at home, with a concussion, with our family doctor, along with my mother and father standing over me. I was ordered to stay at home for six weeks because of the concussion.

First grade ended, and I found myself in second grade. Little did I know what the valley of life meant. I was unable to keep up with my classmates because of a learning disability brought on by the fall.

At the end of that school year, I learned that I would have to take the second grade next school year. I remember to this day my fellow classmates making fun of me, not only because of my poor grades, but also because it was quite apparent that my development had slowed my physical growth in height and weight.

Might I note that my parents were always very supportive of me, especially my mother, who heard my cries and listened to my prayers almost every night. Also, my brother made sure I was not picked on if he was around at that time.

I would be starting second grade in the fall. This year was just more of a repeat of grade 1, but worse. Maybe it was because I was learning what it was to have feelings—the feeling of knowing what it was like living each day with embarrassment, to be lonely and ashamed, to have a low self-esteem, to be a loser and deeply hurt.

About this time, my mother taught me the importance of knowing God and the strength through praying in Jesus Christ's name. I now know, without question, that it was Jesus who helped me through those hard and very difficult times. I remember one night when I was lying in bed crying, grieving, my mother came in with a gift and gave it to me. It was a new white leather-covered King James Version Bible. I tried very hard to read it, but it seemed to take me forever to get through the book of Genesis.

It was at this time when God seemed to say that he would always be at my side. My journey with Jesus began.

After being in the second grade twice, I moved on to the third grade. This year was even worse than the first and second year put together. The learning requirements were much more emphasized, and I failed in each one of the lessons. It was during this year that I had a teacher named Mrs. Whitney, who supported me and encouraged me to stay with it, for the day would come when I would succeed at whatever I wanted to accomplish.

Because of the importance of meeting the requirements needed in third grade, which I was unable to do, it was decided that I would have to take third grade again. One year went into another. The fourth, fifth, and sixth grades did not go much better. I was able to pass the fourth, fifth, and sixth grades, which was not easy, but I did fill the needed requirements.

Then came junior high school—oh, was I scared. But as I look back at that time, it was then that I began to feel God's strength that he gave me to forge ahead, knowing Christ would be at my side, piloting my future. He gave me a new, strong inner strength to succeed at whatever I would set out to do.

In seventh and eighth grades, I began to feel better and stronger about myself. Yes, I had a few Fs, with Ds, Cs, and occasional Bs, and sometimes even As, which gave me great pleasure.

It was at the beginning of ninth grade that I made up my mind that I would get on the honor roll before I would graduate from high school, and with God's help, that is what I did.

On to high school; this was the time I decided what I wanted to do after high school graduation, and that was to become a teacher. I did graduate, not at the top of my class, but I did graduate the spring of 1962, cap, gown, and the works. Lots of pictures were taken. My wonderful mother and father were so proud of me. I think it might have been the first time, although they never said it was.

At that time, the then called Ball State Teachers College was one of the best teacher colleges in the state of Indiana, and their freshman requirements for state applicants were not as high as the out-of-state requirements. I did have to take one semester of advanced English and mathematics from my high school to meet BSTC's requirements. I did not let my pride, being back with high school students, stop me. I went on to BSTC in the fall of 1963.

I remember so clearly when my parents dropped me off at the dorm. I watched their car leave until I could no longer see it. I knew then that with God's help, it was up to me, with him guiding me, to make my dream of becoming a teacher a reality. I could not let myself and, more importantly, my parents down.

As the months and years went by, with long hours of studying and determination during the four and a half years, now Ball State University had produced a teacher with a degree in education. Was I proud, or what?

I sent my résumé to the South Bend School Corporation and signed a contract with them within two weeks. I was assigned to Coqwillard Junior High School in the industrial education department.

This was what I waited so long for, and I loved every minute of it.

I was living at home with my parents, which enabled me to afford a new car, new clothes, to travel, and more importantly, the peace of mind that I had succeeded to live out my dream.

What more could a twenty-four-year-old single man want?

I had been a loner all my life and was happy to be one—that is, I thought I was. It was at this time that my father, along with my brother, had started a successful machine tool business, which seemed to grow in size overnight.

Its growth and success enabled my parents to buy a summer home on Beaver Island, Michigan. This made it possible for me to spend my summers at the island, along with my little dog Shelly. It was a log cabin nestled in trees on the east side of the island.

It was on this island that I was able to spend long hours of quiet time with God. I would sit on the rocky shoreline just a few hundred feet north of our cabin. It was on these occasions that I began to just think about the relationship of the Holy Trinity—the Father, the Son, and the Holy Spirit.

What was it that kept nagging me for the answer as to what that really meant? When I would return home, this question would be lost in my daily lifestyle.

It was on my daily walks on the beautiful beach in front of our cabin, with its blue water lapping on the white-sand beach, that God seemed to say to me, "Don, wouldn't it be nice to share all this with someone?" That never really bothered me much in the past. Oh, sure, from time to time, I thought it would be nice to date some young lady and take her to special events when I would return home from the island.

Returning from the island in the fall of 1970 marked the beginning of another school year. It was a tradition that teachers that were new to the school had to start a week before the other teachers had to report back to work. We all met in the school auditorium on the first day back to meet the other new teachers and to tell of what we did during the summer months. I was a little late in entering the room, so there was only a seat or two not taken.

I sat down and looked across the table, and there was the most beautiful young history teacher sitting in front of me. She had blond hair done up in the back and beautiful blue eyes. She was dressed in a red-and-white striped dress. After we each shared our past summers with each other, I knew right then and there Susan was the one that God had chosen for me from the day I was born. She was not only beautiful but also very intelligent.

Susan and I dated for seven months, and yes, we had our differences, but we worked through them. I knew it was time to ask her to marry me! That I did, and she said yes. Wow, that was the most wonderful, wonderful day of my life.

We were married on December 4, 1971, and we honeymooned for two weeks in Hawaii. Later we were blessed with three healthy sons. All my prayers had been answered, and I thanked God for everything he was blessing us with.

It was at this time when I fell into the trap of materialism. I was starting to see what money had bought my parents and brother—expensive homes, cars, airplanes, businesses. Everything looked fine on the outside, but inside they were not.

It was also at this time we both agreed that a change had to be made, and soon. Ever since those quiet times with God on Beaver Island, I hadn't thought much more about the relationship between Father, the Son, and the Holy Spirit.

In the summer of 1985, we flew out Keystone, Colorado, for a three-week vacation with the intention that Susan and I would ask Christ to help us and guide us into our future.

I would sit out in front of our rented villa with my Bible, praying that God would lead us in the right direction and guide our family into the future. I knew I had to make a career change, but what?

I asked God to help me make that right decision. I believed, and always will believe, that if we sincerely ask God to take control of our lives and truly believe it in our hearts, he will and does. It may not be in the timeframe or outcome we had hoped for, but it will be given to us.

Might I note, now that I think back on it, I subconsciously wanted to stay in control.

The answer was for us to own our own business. But what kind? Having a past with tools and machinery, I believe it was having a hardware store of our own. The one I always dreamed of having was a 103-year-old hardware store in our hometown of Elkhart named Sunthimer's Hardware. The store had been in the same family since its beginning. The owner was in his middle seventies, so I was hoping and praying he would sell.

I called him the next day and asked if he would be interested, and he said he would think it over and let me know.

Yes, I prayed he would, because now that I think about it, that's what *I* wanted. It never entered my mind if that was what God wanted. But maybe it was!

The next day the owner called me and said he would be interested. Three weeks later, an agreement was made, the contract signed. Susan and I and the boys were now in the hardware business. Oh, did I praise God for another mountain peak, another dream come true. I knew this was where God had planned for me to be since the beginning of time. I made it—what more could I ever want or ask for? Susan worked in the office, and the three boys worked cleaning and helping with the different needs of the store.

The store was located on the corner of High Street and Main Street in downtown Elkhart, Indiana. It had the 103-year-old squeaky wooden floors, oak pullout product drawer bins, weighing scales, and all. The store had built up a great customer base, including all of Elkhart's utility customers, industrial accounts, and street customers.

All went fine for the first two years, until the city decided that the main street should be replaced, making it impossible to cross from the west side to the east side, which was where the store happened to be.

We did not realize how this would affect our customer base, which included not only off-the-street customers but also the longtime business accounts that had been built up through many years. Might I also bring up that just before the city had made known they had this project in mind, we purchased the building and corner property from the seller.

From that time on, we noticed our account receivables were growing less and less by the month. I prayed, "Oh, God, how could you let this happen? Why? I thought it was your will." Again, it was my will; he was answering.

This began to become noticeable by us not being able to restock shelves, which had a negative domino effect. Did I pray? I prayed like I had never prayed before! I truly believed that God would make things work out.

During this time, I had become friends with a Christian who had been after me for some time to join him at the weekly Businessmen's Committee Breakfast. I thought, why not, what do I have to lose?

To my surprise, there were some forty men attending weekly. We had prayers and breakfast, and then the leader asked what concerns we each had. Most of these men were business owners I had known, and I thought they had life just the way they wanted. We would then pair up and pray for each other's concerns, and believe me, we all had them.

It was during these meetings that I also befriended two very successful Christian businessmen who knew and understood what my situation was and what my family and I were going through.

One of these men and his wife had mentored many couples in the past, and knowing Susan and me being under great stress, they invited us to go through the Christian Businessmen's

Committee's study called First Steps at their home; this we did on a weekly basis.

After one full year of completing this wonderful study, we were ready to move on with following God's will and *not* mine.

This was about the time when I had the most life-changing experience in my Christian walk in finding the meaning of the Trinity after so many years of searching.

This truly happened inside the walls of Sunthimer's Hardware.

First, let me explain the layout of the old store. It sat on the northeast corner of Main Street, which ran north to south, and Lexington Street, which ran east to west on a hill. The hill started its descent from the top of the stairway to the southeast corner of the store, which was two-hundred-plus feet to that corner where the backdoor of the basement opened to the rear customer parking lot.

The floor plan of the store was as follows: The ground level (first floor) was the selling floor on the Main Street level, and the basement was on the back parking lot level. There was a sixty-foot-long walkway from the backdoor to a five-foot-wide stairway that went up to the second floor sales area. This stairway had a midlevel landing, which was six feet in length. At the very top of the stairway was the U-shaped checkout counter where the cash registers were located. This was no more than six feet away from the top step, and on each side of the stairway on ground level were a two-and-a-half-foot-high railings.

On a dark, cold, foggy, rainy evening in late November of 1987, just before our 5:00 p.m. closing time, two of my employees and I were talking and were more than ready to lock the doors when two men walked up those back stairs. Mind you, the evening was very cold and rainy, and we had no customers after 4:00 p.m.

One man was tall and well-built, dressed in brown slacks with a brown-and-tan checkered lumber jacket. The other man was small in stature, dressed in a dark-blue utility overall suit, like a gas station tenant back then. The larger man led, with the smaller man, with his hands in his pockets, walking up the stairs. I could not remember ever seeing anyone do that because of the danger of falling or tripping on the long flight of stairs.

Both men were clean, well shaven, with up-to-date haircuts. The larger man walked over to the counter. I was behind the counter facing east, and my two employees facing to the left outside the counter. The smaller man, with his hands still in his pockets, with the bluest eyes I have ever, ever seen, stood at the top and to the right of the left side railing.

I asked the larger man how I could help him. He asked if we had hinges, and I said yes. With my two employees listening, he asked if I believed in angels, which caught me off guard. Being a little bit embarrassed in front of my two employees, I had to say, "Yes, I do." I also asked him if he did, and he replied, "Oh yes, I do."

At that point, my two employees left for the back room to get ready to leave for the night. I had the feeling they had not preferred to be part of that conversation.

I took the man over to the hinges and asked him what type of hinge he had in mind. Without saying anything, he picked out one small two-inch brass hinge. I asked him if he only needed one. He said yes, which seemed strange to me at that time, because I usually always sold them in pairs.

I looked over at the smaller man in blue. He had not moved, and his hands were still in his pockets. He also never stopped staring at me. Again, strange.

The man in the checkered jacket and I walked back to the counter to check out, and while I was ringing him up, he brought up the subject of angels again. He said I should always believe in angels, because in an experience he had years back when he owned a fueling station, which was not doing well, he and his sons were visited by an angel, who said they would be able to get through this difficult time in their lives.

At this time, I looked over at the man in blue still staring at me, with his hands in his pockets, not ever saying a word.

The man in the checkered jacket thanked me and said "Always keep believing" as he descended the stairs a few steps in front the man in blue, still with his hands in his pockets. When he said his last words, I had started back to the counter, and it suddenly struck me.

I realized who they were. I leaped to the top of the stairs; they could not possibly be able to get below the six-foot midstair landing. They had just disappeared. I flew down the stairs, and there was no one in that long walkway. I ran as fast as I could for the door, ran outside, looking left and right, up and down the street. They had literally disappeared.

I got on my knees and cried for I don't remember how long, and I thanked God for visiting me. For I know without question that I was visited by an angel and the man in blue with his hands in his pockets, with those beautiful blue eyes, was Jesus Christ himself.

Seek and You Shall Find

Since then, I have searched and prayed for an answer as to why the angel bought only one small hinge. In my heart, I believe God has given me the answer to my prayer.

He reminded me of the verse in the Bible, in Matthew 7:7: "Ask, and it will be given to you; seek, and you will find; knock, and it will be opened to you." I kept asking and searching for years, not just for what has happened to me in the past, but for deeper understanding of what the future held for me and my beautiful family.

A hinge is a device holding two parts, held together by a single pin, which allows one half to be able to work together with the other half.

What God has told me is that man is on half of the hinge of life, and the Trinity (Father, Son, and Holy Spirit) is on the other, and they are held together by angels, being the pin. Revelation 3:1 suggests that he (Jesus) is so closely united with angels that it is through their presence everywhere, and them reporting back to him, that he is able to know always.

I knew the answer had to be in the Holy Bible. A careful study will reveal that the NT activity of angels usually revolves around the ministry of Jesus and the establishment of his church on earth. They "minister," referring to their "serviceable labor, assistance."

They are ministering spirits, or heavenly assistances, who are continually active today in building the body of Christ—advancing the ministry of Jesus and the building of his church.

Throughout the scriptures, from Genesis through Revelation, angels have been the communicators between the Trinity and mankind.

The following verses are all from the Old Testament and the New Testament, which are just a few examples where angels are so much a part of God's creation.

The Old Testament

Now the Angel of the Lord Sarai by a spring of water in the wilderness, by the spring on the way to Shur. (Gen. 16:7)

The Angel "who has redeemed me from all evil." (Gen. 48:16)

Behold, I send an Angel before you to keep you in the way and to bring you into place which I have prepared. (Exod. 23:20)

Now the donkey saw the Angel of the Lord standing in the way with the drawn sword in His hand. (Num. 22:23)

Now Gideon perceived that He was the Angel of the LORD. So Gideon said "Alas, O LORD GOD! For I have seen the Angel of the LORD face to face." (Judg. 6:22)

Then Manoah said to the Angel of the LORD, "What is Your name, that when Your words come to pass we may honor You?" (Judg. 13:17)

Then Achish answered and said to David, "I know that you are good in my sight as an angel of God." (1 Sam. 29:9)

And the angel stretched out His hand over Jerusalem to destroy it, the Lord relented from the destruction, and said to the angel who was destroying the people, "It is enough; now restrain your hand." And the angel of the LORD was by the threshing floor of Araunah the Jedusite. (2 Sam. 24:16)

And it came to pass on a certain night that the angel of the LORD went out, and killed in the camp of the Assyrians one hundred and eighty-five thousand; and when the people arose early in the morning, there were corpses, all dead. (2 Kings 19:35)

In that day the Lord will defend the inhabitants of Jerusalem; the one who is feeble among them in that day shall be like David, and the house of David shall be like God, like the Angel of the LORD before them. (Zech. 12:8)

The New Testament

While Joseph thought about these things behold, an angel of the Lord appeared to him in a dream, saying, "Joseph, son of David, do not be afraid to take you to Mary your wife, for that which is conceived in her is the Holy Spirit." (Matt. 1:20)

And behold there was a great earthquake, for an angel of the LORD descended from heaven, and came and rolled back stone from the door, and sat on it. (Matt. 28.2)

Then an angel of the LORD appeared to him, standing on the right side of the altar of incense. (Luke 1:11)

And behold an angel of the Lord stood before them, and the glory of the Lord shone around them, and they were greatly afraid. (Luke 2:9)

Then an angel appeared to him from heaven, strengthening him. (Luke 22:43)

Therefore the people who stood by and heard it said that it had thundered. Others said an angel has spoken to Him. (John 5:4)

But that night an angel of the Lord opened the prison doors and brought out. (Acts 5:19)

This Moses whom they rejected, saying, "Who made you a ruler and a judge?" is the one God sent to be ruler and a deliverer by the hand of the Angel who appeared to him in the bush. (Acts 7:35)

Then immediately an angel of the Lord struck him, because he did not give glory to God. And he was eaten by worms and died." (Acts 12:23)

Then I saw a strong angel proclaiming with aloud voice, "Who is worthy to open the scroll and to loosen its seals?" (Rev. 5:2)

Then I saw an angel standing in the sun; and he cried with a loud voice, saying to all the birds that fly in the mist of heaven, "Come and gather together for the supper of the great God." (Rev. 19:17)

I, Jesus, have sent my angel to testify to you these things in the churches. I am the Root and the Offspring of David, the Bright and Morning Star. (Rev. 22:16)

During this time, Susan and I knew we had to start downsizing our worldly way of life in order to pay our bills. We knew that it was God's will that we pay all bills that we had committed ourselves to do so. This meant selling our five-bedroom house, my grandmother's 1953 Oldsmobile, my violin, my piano, and so on.

All this time, my wonderful Susan, God love her, never, never complained. Without God and the wonderful gift of Susan in my life, I would have ended the hell I was going through, and I was very close in carrying it through.

As I grew in my faith journey, it became apparent to me that all this time, I was still trying to do things my way. I knew that I had to spend much more time in scripture to seek the answers as to why—why there was so much of my life spent in one valley after another.

In order to save the hardware store, the decision was to try to sell the property downtown and move Sunthimer's business to another location in a strip mall, which was two miles away at a busy intersection where a bridge that joined the north side of the river to the south side had been built in front of the river dam.

I prayed—oh, did I pray—that by some remote chance, a buyer would come along and buy the old building and property. And, lo and behold, the owner of a drugstore half a block away heard that it was for sale and bought it for the price it was bought.

We were able to work a rent price out with the owner of the strip mall and move the inventory to the new location at that busy intersection. Right after our grand opening, we noticed many of our older customers returning, along with new customers that added to our customer list.

After a year and half at that location, the government bridge inspection people came in town to inspect all bridges in the city and decided that our bridge had to be replaced. To all of us locals, this bridge was always called the Dam Bridge, and now it should be shut down for a two-year repair project. (The name of the bridge took on a new meaning.)

On the day it closed, we noticed right away that our account receivables were lesser by each passing day. I had to lay off all employees, all but my store manager, who stuck with me to the end, and without pay, by his own choosing.

After seven years, my dream of having our own hardware store was over. We were head-deep in debt to the bank and out of work. We were able to sell the assets to another local hardware west of town. Sunthimer's Hardware was no longer. I had failed again and was in another valley.

Over the next few years, I went back to work at the family's machine tool company until it too, eventually, closed its doors.

It was at this time that I decided to start my own sales representative business called OSI, which stood for Outsourcing with Integrity." It did quite well for the next few years.

It took nearly eight years to pay back all the debt that we owed to the bank. We gave them our word that we would do so, and we did 100 percent! OSI did quite well, but not well enough to keep up with the travel expenses along with other expenses of keeping our household expenses current. It was decided that it was time to close OSI and search for something with a steady income and good benefits.

It wasn't a week after the closing when out of nowhere, the industrial education director for the South Bend School Corporation called me and asked if I would be interested in taking over the industrial education department at Riley High School in South Bend, Indiana, for one year.

Wow, did this ever come at the right time! My prayers had been answered.

One morning, the strangest thing happened while I was getting ready for work. It was routine for me to shower and shave. While lathering my face with shaving cream, I was startled by a loud popping sound like a small firecracker from out of nowhere! I looked down, and the small wooden cross I had worn around my neck for years was broken into three pieces.

I asked God to please give me the answer as to why this had happened to me—what was he trying to tell me?

As time went by, I was still asking why. I now believe that God has given me the answer, because of the experience I had at the old hardware store with the angel buying just one small hinge. The upper right center piece signified the angel, with one arm signifying God, Jesus, and the Holy Spirit, and the other arm signifying man.

At the end of that year of teaching, I decided to work for Lowe's Home Center, where I still work at to this day. Susan went to work as a secretary at our church and then went on to become a receptionist at our dentist office for the next ten years. All this time, that foggy, rainy night visit at the old hardware never left my mind. What was God still trying to tell me?

Our faith in Jesus Christ began to take on a new meaning, and it grew and was strengthened.

God was still working in my heart to let me learn and know the true depth of what it means to have the Trinity deep and alive within our hearts and minds. All this time, I shared these thoughts with Susan. We grew together.

Oh yes, after selling our beautiful home, we rented a small lake cottage that provided us with two bedrooms—one for Susan and me and one upstairs room large enough for the three boys.

After six years, we were able to buy a small house in our old neighborhood. It felt great.

It was about this time when the boys were ready to go out on their own. Justin was one of the first to marry. He married Kristy, our daughter-in-law, who gave us two beautiful grandchildren, Austin and Averi.

It was at this time in our lives in early 2006 that Susan and I started to get serious about the future and how we wanted to spend the rest of our lives together as we grew older.

Susan was still working for the dentist office, and I with Lowes, when she began not feeling well, weak, losing energy. It was decided that she should make an appointment with her doctor to have a physical.

Part of that physical was to have her colon checked for any polyps, which could turn into cancerous tumors. What they found was a large mass on the left side of the colon. It was decided that she spend the night, and the surgery would be scheduled the next morning.

I had very little sleep that night, praying that the tumor would not be cancerous.

After a sleepless night, morning came, and I headed for the hospital, where I was asked by the doctor to wait in the waiting room until the surgery was over and he would come in and talk to me. Two and a half hours later, he returned to the waiting room and sat with me and told me that the tumor was cancerous and that she would have to have chemotherapy treatments in the weeks to come.

I waited until Susan was out of the recovery room, followed her to her room, where we talked and prayed that God would please take the cancer from her body.

After leaving her that evening, I drove for miles crying, asking God why. "Why? How could you let this happen to Susan?" We were believers in Jesus Christ, always had been, and we always prayed for good health and safety for our family and friends. "After all we had been through, now this! Why this?"

Weeks and months went by with the chemo treatments, the waiting for the next MRI to be taken, and praying that results would show her clear of the cancer. The results were not good. They showed that there was another tumor that had developed on the other side of her colon and had invaded her lymph nodes around her stomach area.

The second surgery was scheduled later that afternoon, which lasted some four hours.

Again, after the surgery, the doctor met me in the waiting room and said they had removed the tumor, and she would have to have more chemotherapy treatments.

The drive from the Goshen Hospital was only twelve miles from our home, but that trip seemed like a hundred miles.

After arriving home, I went to the basement so Susan could not hear me. I again cried, asking God why. Why?

Down deep in my heart, I seemed to know that my beloved Susan and I would not be growing old together. I am quite sure that Susan knew from the beginning that we would not, but she never said anything to me to that effect.

All this time, I never questioned that God would answer my prayers and heal her of the cancer. I knew that having our deep belief in God was what would get both of us through this bad dream we had been living.

On a beautiful sunny day in fall, we had lunch at our dining room. The sun was shining brightly through the window, and Susan appeared to me to look so beautiful that I asked her if I could take her picture. With reluctance, she said yes. Weeks later, I came across the picture I had taken of her. I knew right then it was God's timing, that I must face the reality that he had other plans for Susan and was going to be calling her home to live with him in paradise.

I was sure it must have been very noticeable to others that she was becoming weaker and weaker with the loss of weight and becoming very frail.

The dreadful moment came when it was suggested that I call hospice home care to come to the house to help Susan with her personal needs, and that I did. They were so helpful and kind, very sensitive to her needs and mine also.

I felt in my heart the night before the Lord called her to live in paradise with him that it would be our last night to fall to asleep together, even though she slept in a hospital bed that was brought into our bedroom. There, I fell asleep, holding her in my arms until sunrise.

Still having hope that God would heal my sweetheart, on the evening of December 14, 2008, while I was alone with Susan, I knew the end of this journey was soon to come. I went to get a white Easter candle with a cross on it and lit it beside Susan. For that last week, she held a rugged small wooden plum cross on her left hand, which had been given to her, never letting loose.

I held her right hand in mine, and I prayed that the Lord would take Susan into his arms and carry her to heaven. After saying amen, I opened my eyes, and I could clearly see that my prayer had been answered. The candle flame went out, with the smoke going straight up, and the wooden plum cross was lying on the sheet below her hand. (No breeze of any kind was in the room to put out the candle.)

It's been some time since I have sat down at my computer to try to consolidate my feelings, thoughts, emotions, and journey with Christ. When I turned seventy on July 19, 2012, it came to me—yes, I really was seventy years old, and my life here on earth will sometime end too.

In these last few months, I have found myself to be depressed and lonely because I have now come to realize and accept that my Susan has gone to live with Christ in heaven, and I will have to wait until the Lord calls me home to be with her again.

I prayed in earnest for God to help me overcome this darkness I was living in and to be happy again until that day came.

I knew deep within my heart that the answer had to be in the Holy Bible. I knew that I had to make a stronger, sincere effort and commitment to God in truly wanting to know the true answer to my prayer of understanding the meaning of having the Holy Trinity living within me.

When I look back, praying in those quiet moments, acknowledging the Father, Son, and Holy Spirit, I never really acknowledged the Holy Spirit and how angels fit into our lives, again not giving them much thought. I guess I believed knowing the Father and Son was all I really needed.

I often look back on my life and realize that the things I prayed for, God had answered—not only things, but also places I wanted to visit and explore. And that is what I did: the ancient pyramids in Mexico; hot air ballooning for miles along the Continental Divide; taking a Mediterranean cruise visiting different counties and their culture; cruising to Alaska where I walked on a glacier, drove a dog sled, and rode in a helicopter between the great snow-capped mountains of Alaska; taking my grandson Austin on a Caribbean cruise, where we went paragliding, waterfall climbing, cave exploring, rock climbing, and snorkeling.

God kept reminding me that as a believer, I have the Holy Spirit living, truly living, within me and reminding me of what it really means. Deep within my heart, I kept asking, "What did it mean? What did it mean?"

As I have said before, I knew the only place to find that answer had to be the Bible and that I would have to expand my study to find it. It was then that I studied as much literature as I could find on the Holy Spirit, the Holy Bible being the main source.

From the beginning in Genesis 1:2 through Revelation 22:21, the Holy Spirit was ever so involved, so active in the creation of God's world, in believers. As it is said in the book of John 14:16–17, Jesus made the promise to his disciples that he would leave them with another helper: "And I will pray to the Father, and He will give you another Helper, that may abide with you forever . . . the Spirit of truth, whom the world cannot receive, because it never sees Him nor knows Him; but you know Him, for He dwells with you and will be in you."

Scripture says to keep asking, seeking, and knocking, and the door will be opened.

Jesus's last words to his disciples before his crucifixion concerning the Holy Spirit's ministry, which he said in John 14:25–26, were, "I still have many things to say to you, but you cannot bear them now. However when He, the Spirit of truth, has come, He will guide you into all truth; for He will not speak on His own authority, but whatever He hears He will speak; and He will tell you things to come. He will glorify Me, for He will take of what is Mine and declare it to you."

The book of Luke 11:9–13 says, "So I say to you, ask, and it will be given to you; seek and you will fine; knock, and it will be opened to you. For anyone that asks receives, and he who seeks finds, and to him who knocks it will be opened. If a son asks for bread from any father among you, will he give him a stone? Or if he asks for a fish, will he give him a serpent instead of a fish? Or if he asks for an egg, will he offer him a scorpion? If you then, being evil, know how to give good gifts to your children, how much more will your Father give the Holy Spirit to those who ask Him!"

Again, I have asked God to help me understand what this really meant, how this would change my life to live up to his will. "Ask and it will be given to you, seek and you will find; knock and the door will be open to you" (Matt. 7:7).

I keep reminding myself of what he said in John 14:16–17, when he left his disciples, as is noted previously, "I will give you another Helper, that may abide with you forever."

I realize that if I really believed in God's Word, I should realize that what he says *must* be the truth! I believe my angel gave me the message to really think about who the Holy Spirit is, and what difference he would make in my life and is doing in my life now.

I come to know that if I truly want to be happy while I am still living on this earth, the answer must be in God's Word, the

Holy Bible. (Let me mention, the Bible I study from is the New Spirit-Filled Life Bible, which was given to me by Susan's sister Donna on June 5, 2007, at the time Susan was going through her cancer treatments.

What keeps coming back to me again and again is that it must be the Holy Spirit and the gift he holds in his hands for all men to have, just for the asking. That is the fruit of the Spirit: love, joy, peace, patience, kindness, goodness, faithfulness, gentleness, and self-control.

Always before, when I would see these words, they were just words. I never really gave them any deep thought as to what they really meant. Oh yes, I knew what the words were and their meaning from my visual sight of the words, but that was as far as it went.

I read in David Jeremiah's book *God in You* that there are three kinds of people who go to church.

First, there are "those who come to church but don't know the Lord at all. The Holy Spirit doesn't live within them, so they can't be filled with Him."

Second, there are "people who are Christians, and the Holy Spirit lives within them, but they've never given Him control of their life. They're believers, but they don't live a very Christian life while living on a carnal level."

Third are those who have consciously and knowingly given over their lives to the Holy Spirit's control. They live every day with the knowledge that there is a power within them, the third person of the Trinity, who controls their life and destiny.

In wanting to know in my heart what God was trying to teach me, again I felt that I should try to learn more and more and become much better acquainted with who the Holy Spirit is and what his mission is in the Trinity.

I know that God, along with the Holy Spirit, created the entire universe, with all the plants and with its endless space. Genesis 1:2 says, "The Spirit of God was hovering over the face of the waters." We find the Spirit involved in the Creation. The Holy Spirit also worked in Joseph, a fact obvious to Pharaoh, as stated in Genesis 41:38: "Can we find such a one as this, a man in whom is the spirit of God?" First Thessalonians 1:5–6 says, "For the gospel did not come to you in word only, but also in power, and in the Holy Spirit, and in much assurance, as you know what kind of men we were among you for your sake. And you became followers of us, and of the Lord, having received the word much affliction, with joy of the Holy Spirit."

I asked myself, what does the Bible mean when it says to be filled with the Spirit? I looked at different verses in the Bible such as the following:

Scripture says in 1 Thessalonians 5:16–18, "Rejoice, and without ceasing, in everything give thanks." How can I, or anybody, live up to that?

Scripture says in Ephesians 4:2, "Be completely humble and gentle." Oh, how could I do that?

Scripture says in 2 Corinthians 10:5, "Take captive every thought to make it obedient to Christ." Every thought? How could I ever do that?

Scripture says in Matthew 5:44, "Do good to those who hate you, and pray for those who spitefully use you and persecute you." Are you kidding me?

I now feel deep within my heart that if I do not keep in close, consistent contact with the Holy Spirit in the name of Jesus each day I'm given on this earth, I will not be able to live up to God's will that he has for me. It is an ongoing process.

Being filled with the Holy Spirit has to begin with desire. I had to pray deep within my heart and soul for a long-lasting, deep, and sincere desire to want to live in God's will for me to be truly happy.

I found six meanings of *desire*: (1) "express a desire for," (2) "feel or have the desire to want strongly," (3) "an inclination to want things," (4) "expect and wish," (5) "something that is desired," and (6) "the feeling that accompanies an unsatisfied state."

Without acknowledging the Holy Spirit and the fruit of life he holds just for the asking in Jesus's name, true happiness cannot be possible. We can do nothing without the Lord, and it is only as we remain in him that we bear any fruit (John 15:5). Galatians 5:22–23 says, "The fruit of the Spirit is love, joy peace, patience, kindness, goodness, faithfulness, and self-control. Against such things there is no law."

Oh, sure, short spurts of happiness happen often, but they do not last for a length of time. It's not true lasting happiness!

I believe with all my heart that without a true, sincere will to recognize the Holy Spirit that is just for the asking, it is impossible to live a life in peace and happiness. "The fruit of the Spirit are the Holy Spirit's fruit found in the life of the believer. We can do nothing without the Lord, and it is only as we remain in Him that we bear any fruit" (John 15:5). "Again the fruit are love, joy, peace, patience, kindness, goodness, faithfulness, gentleness, and self-control" (Gal. 5:22–23).

The fruit of the Spirit can be summed up in love. Love sums up the whole law and the prophets (Gal 5:14). Love is the most excellent way (1 Cor. 13:31). Love is proven true by its actions, not by feelings (1 Cor. 13:4–7).

Love is the primary form of the fruit and is listed first. The others that follow may be understood as the different ways in which the fruit of love manifests itself.

Peace is love resting.

Patience is love forbearing.

Kindness is love serving.

Goodness is love seeking the best for others.

Faithfulness is love keeping its promises.

Gentleness is love ministering to the hurts of others.

Self-control is love in control.

I have come to realize that just because a person has repented of his sins and claimed salvation in Christ does not mean that his or her whole character has instantly transformed. Yes, it is a very important process of change that has been put into motion, but it may take many years for that change to work out in every area of a person's life as it has in mine.

As for me, I am humbled, because I still have so far to go, and inspired, because I have caught a glimpse of something more beautiful than anything that this world has to offer.

In the words of Paul, "I do not count myself to have apprehended; but one thing I do, forgetting those things which are behind and reaching forward to those things which are ahead, I press toward the goal for the prize of the upward call of God in Christ Jesus."

I cannot think of one person that I know who does not enjoy being happy, rather than being overcome by depression and sadness, which can be brought on by a loss of a loved one, financial reasons, health reasons, possessions—the list goes on and on. Jesus said, "Come to me and take My yoke upon you, and I will fill you with my life." He will fill you with the Holy Spirit. Who is the Holy Spirit? He is Jesus living within you and waiting for you to just ask him, in Jesus's name, in welcoming him to change your heart and soul.

Each one of our lives has been lived on a different path than anyone else's. That is why change may arrive very quietly, or it may take time, as it did for me, for God to prepare you for that change.

We must remain patient, because our prayers will be answered in time. Don't ever give up your desire to have such a beautiful and wonderful personal relationship with Jesus Christ himself.

Jesus uniquely custom-created this relationship for you only.

Jesus said, "We would know people by their fruits not by their gifts" (Matt. 7:16–23). People will know we are Jesus's disciples by our love (John 13:35). The fruits are evidence of godly character in a disciple's life, because they can only grow out of a life that is dead to the self and that lives by the Spirit (Gal. 5:16, 24, 25).

I know there are so many people in this world, in our neighborhoods, in our own families, and maybe within ourselves, that live day in and day out with the loss of a loved one, loneliness, depression, financial loss, health problems—the list goes on and on!

Everyone wants to be living in peace, and that is only possible by believing in Jesus Christ as the Son of God and recognizing what it means to have the Holy Spirit alive and living within each one of us with the help of our angels.

Through my belief in Jesus since the age of six, I have finally found after seventy-three years that the one and only way to have happiness, which I never really thought possible or ever existed, was just there, living within me all this time.

> Ask and it will be given to you; seek and you will find; knock and the door will be open to you. (Matt. 7:7)

> Seek and you shall find!

Made in the USA
Lexington, KY
13 October 2017